Rita Unger:

An autobiography

In Verse

Published 2017 by arima publishing
www.arimapublishing.com

ISBN 978 1 84549 605 0

Printed and bound in the United Kingdom

Typeset in Garamond

Swirl is an imprint of arima publishing.

arima publishing
ASK House, Northgate Avenue
Bury St Edmunds, Suffolk IP32 6BB
t: (+44) 01284 700321
www.arimapublishing.com

Dedicated
To
My Family and Friends

CONTENTS

FELINE

Their hearts contract
As they pass his neat,
Newly dug grave
At the foot of the garden.
He lies at peace now,
Bathed in the early spring sunshine.
They plan to cover his resting place
With a carpet
Of wild meadow flowers.

He was an extraordinary creature,
Unique, Ubiquitous,
Eccentric,
Universally adored.
Now and then,
One would glance down at him
With affection
As he lay habitually supine,
His placid, silent presence
Comfortably inert.

He, a rotund,
Fluffy, tangled,
Purple rug,
His fur was in constant need
Of grooming and unknotting.

He was omnipresent,
Ever there, Close by,
Always basking contentedly in any company,
Quietly and utterly sociable,
Purring with ecstasy whenever fondled.
One might turn,
And there he would be,
At your feet
Like a faithful bloodhound.

He was the benign, ruling emperor
Of their imposing house,
Padding about it majestically.
He so relished its comforts,
Particularly the fire,
Would head for it when lit
Like a heat-seeking missile,
Stretching out serenely
For solace and warmth,
Hogging the blaze.

He was discreetly
But ferociously territorial,
Guarding his patch,
The substantial garden
With much judicial scrapping,
Defending it ruthlessly.
He led a mysterious,
Altogether secretive,
Nocturnal existence.

Aged just fifteen,
Although elderly in feline years,
He grew suddenly ill,
And just faded away
In a matter of weeks
With the minimum of fuss,
Leaving his owners
Inconsolably stricken with grief,
Barely able to withstand
The sadness of their loss,
His now eternal absence.

Might they ever truly
Cease to mourn his passing?
Perhaps not,
For there will always be the memories,
But doubtless,
The sun shines forever
In moggy heaven,
And there he will be,
Still amiably watching over them,
A sentinel on high.

14/03/2012

RIOT

I stood at the window,
Rooted to the spot with fear.
I watched them riot
As with fevered excitement,
Laughing mirthlessly,
They tore apart my neighbourhood
With little conscience.

There were children,
So young,
Barely out of primary school,
Queueing impatiently,
Waiting to take their turn
To acquire trainers,
A mobile phone.
Women were crawling through the shattered doors
Of Marks & Spencer,
Emerging with armfuls of underwear,
Strolling casually away
As though shopping on an unremarkable day.

Terror turned to ice
As I felt the building shudder.
I was trapped
As they battered the grille
Of a neighbouring jewellers,
And pillaged its stock,
Trashed the shop next door.

Across the street,
Rows of onlookers stood almost motionless,
Only stirring to photograph the scene,
Observing glassy-eyed,
Pruriently,
With voyeuristic pleasure
The destruction unfolding before them.

There was the dread of being torched,
Of course,
The trauma stretching for an eternity,
Although it was but a matter
Of three or four hours.

I emerged later as it quietened,
Eerily,
Thinking it was all over,
But too fearful to go to bed,
And came face to face
With a line of kettled rioters,
Now detained,
Standing obediently in their impromptu prison,
No guilt,
No fear,
Just boredom on their faces.

And what was the cause?
Poverty,
Unemployment,
Anger,
Disempowerment,
Culture,
Criminal intent,
Or merely greed?
Or were they taking back their lives?
There is no answer.

For now,
I just drift in thought,
Still alone,
Subsumed by my ordeal,
And wait for my world to right itself.
And pray
That never again will such trial visit me.
And I grow cold.

12/08/2011

CARE HOME CHILD

As I watched the programme,
Related to his narrative,
I wept,
For each word was expressed
With dignity, intelligence,
Insight,
A moving clarity.
He spoke without heat or anger,
With quiet, questing acceptance.

I was neither abused
Nor neglected,
In fact raised scrupulously,
Nurtured,
Almost cherished.
My carers were a windbreak,
A shelter against the family of my birth,
And their raging, psychotic,
Slaughtering dysfunction.

But there would never be a time
When I would heal,
Become entirely one,
My questions resolved,
For it was too late,
The damage too profound.
The fear too deep.
I grew up with a hole in my heart,
An aching desire to be wanted,
To belong,
But with a conviction that I was unworthy.
That sadness never went away.

I shall carry with me always
The trauma of departure,
Stepping through the gates
Into an unfamiliar,
Utterly alien world,
And finding myself lost in psychological isolation,
A maze of bewilderment.

So as he talked of his time in care
With such simplicity and truth,
And found in the end
His own kind of peace,
Perhaps reached the end of his journey,
I cried,

And my tears at his words
Fell one by one,
Like salted rain.

02/04/2011

THE DEATH OF LOVE

And it was in the air,
A mourning, a desolation.
In supplication crouched,
I bow my head in grief.
Excise this pain, this anguish,
For my weeping heart,
Be of balm,
Of comfort.

But solace be there none,
For in all the world,
There is nought but silence,
No answer,
Just an empty echo in mute reply.

So might the heavens open,
The stars bleed,
And raindrops fall to the Earth like leaden tears,
To wash the arid soil
Of my desultory love.

But no fruit will ripen,
Nor shoot spring forth,
Nor scented flower bloom.
In the garden void of tenderness,
Frail blossom thirsts and dies.

10/03/1998

BLESSINGS OF THE HEART

I reflect upon the era past,
Am touched with a quiet gratitude,
For your compassion,
Empathy.
I muse,
Where fled the years?

As one you waltz to the song of time,
I warmed and soothed
As I bathe in the glow
Of your union bond,
Cradled in your sagacity.
As wellsprings of my heart you run,
Clear,
And pure,
And crystalline.

So I venerate this splendid day,
That He keep you safe
With tender watch,
As you did I,
For here on Earth
His hallowed works you be,
And such resplendent stars
In his provident sky,
You ever radiate.

So, as long as consciousness doth hold,
Its sacred trust,
I safeguard with care
Recall of you,
Thou blessings of my heart.

Dedicated with love to Jack and Esther Rosen MBE, on the occasion of their 90th birthdays and 67th Wedding Anniversary celebration.

19/08/2003

BORN OF THE CHOSEN

The star of the Hebrew Faith has burned undimmed
For more than five millennia.
It underlies the bedrock of my ancient race,
A belief of compassion, majesty and wisdom,
With its tongue so holy,
Its litany of music so moving and glorious,
Its tenets so mystical,
Yet comforting and familiar.
A singular, rigorous way of life for the most devout,
An unquestioned clock
That sets the hour.

Though seldom now I worship,
I was born and raised a Jew,
And so shall I die.
Still it runs deep through my veins,
My heritage.
It colours my consciousness,
My thoughts most profound,
And will be with me to the end of my days,
And beyond.

For what can surpass the pleasure
Of the welcome for the Sabbath Bride,
Her candles glowing softly into the dusk,
Blessed in silence?
Or the rock of the tribe,
Joyously gathered together,
Young and old,
As they break their bread,
And praise the Almighty in song?
The warmth of belonging to a caste unique.

Such closeness of family I rarely encounter,
Being left with few kin,
Just glimpses of others of my Faith,
Through the windows of their strength
Born of affinity,
Bonded together by familial ties
As they celebrate or meet in prayer.
But still my People,
And deep in my heart is the comfort
That the door stands ever open,
Should I elect to enter.

16/09/2000

CARAPACE

What is to come,
I ask with apprehension.
I know little of what forebodes,
What holds,
Other than the surety
That in the ascendant await dust and ash,
But am daunted by this world
For you so fair,
It bites hostile and uncertain,
Its sweetness dilute.

I kneel upon the sideline,
Observing your quicksilver,
Buoyant tread,
Such as I should wish,
And I ache within.
Each tiny,
Insubstantial matter breaks my bones,
My carapace so fragile
And so fine.

And now
I gather resolution as I spin,
Spiralling from one to another,
So genuflected
I lie sunken.
Will you listen to my heartache,
Shake hard your head in helpless pity,
Then walk away.
Shall I inward gaze,
At the shrinking of my soul,
Perhaps in certain knowledge
That to the very end,
I rise or fall alone.

10/03/2003

MAELSTROM

On that day,
We were caught elliptically in the maelstrom,
Venn diagrams,
Circles overlapping,
Linked by shared perception.

With horror
I watched the unfolding of events,
Experienced nauseous disbelief
At the atrocity unleashed,
Choked on the visceral evil
Of such barbarism.

I am now but one of many,
Now watchfully anxious,
Fearful of their retribution,
A citizen of a flawed
Yet mighty metropolis
As were a number who perished.

The insane,
Incomprehensible carnage
Was enacted in obeisance,
But would a compassionate, loving deity
Desire brutal sacrifice,
Command such pitiless slaughter,
Incite black hatred,
Sadistic bloodlust.

Call for culling of the innocent
With baying triumph.
What satanic nature of men
Could the perpetrators be,
To generate such deeds?

02/08/2005

EVENTIDE

An Autumn love,
A quiet affection,
A sanguine reflection of the soul
In the still of one's years,
Is a rare and priceless gift,
A bejewelled offering.

To be blessed
With such tender attachment
Is an elegant delight,
Perhaps accompanied
By a modicum of doubt,
Hesitant pleasure,
Nevertheless,
It softly cossets the heart,
Mellifluously lightens the spirit.

Those who alight upon this gentle grace
Of a later, measured,
Yet perfect romance,
Might be nourished and kindled
By such emollient flame.

For it anoints with a serenity
They never aspired to find,
And enfolds them safe and close
Within the matrix
Of a douce and dancing companionship,
Throughout the luminous dusk,
The genteel eventide
Of their days.

20/12/2010

THE SPECTRE OF DEMENTIA

I drift inexorably
Toward the other side of silence,
The gateway,
The portal to oblivion.
I tread with uncertainty now,
Trepidation,
As I begin to forget,
Your face,
Your name.

How swiftly might I slip
Into the morass of the twilight years
Is a matter for conjecture,
Falling,
Falling,
Devoured whole,
Or perhaps in part,
Atom by atom.

I shall rage powerfully,
If with impotence,
As I choke on obfuscation,
Should fight the good fight,
But the remnant of a dying, morbid consciousness
Would be ground to abstraction,
Ensnared by the relentless bite
Of sabre-toothed darkness,
The spectre of dementia.

19/11/2010

GIFT OF LIFE

Little does it serve to weep
For that which might have been,
To cast one's thoughts with anguish
Back upon the empty years,
Nor grieve and sorrow
For the loss of a childhood,
And the dark
And bitter struggle of maturity.

I lost my passage through the wilderness
For so long,
A pitiless journey.
But although annihilated
By the unequal battle to survive,
Draw another breath,
Still abide I here
To relate my story,
And bestow my heart in love.

Stand I now upon the threshold
Of my dawn,
And with enlightenment,
Comes the realisation
That never shall I find the panacea,
However long I search,
Nor be formed anew,
For the rainbow has no end.
As I was born,
So shall I die.

So I must make the choice,
Though there be none,
To steel the soul,
Or face defeat.
For life is a gift
Bequeathed yet once,
And all there will ever be.

29/02/2000

GRIEF

Bast,
Fierce guardian angel,
Cloak of sandstone,
Jet,
And ice,
Eyes of obsidian.

Still,
Lithe,
Noble,
Graceful,
With the pride of a queen,
Her purr next my ear
A rockfall in a canyon.

Love laid at my feet
Like a bird.
Now you sail the waters
Of Osiris,
Part of me
Doth also sleep.

1989

HYMN OF THE EARTH

It was early morning,
So blessed a time,
As sharp and clean as a glass of clear spring water.
One sensed a pleasurable wildness to the coming day,
Yet a calm,
An intense tranquillity,
As the bees hazed,
And the dew dried on the springing grass,
Rising as mist into the air.
It was June,
Summer's height,
And all was vibrant beneath the sun.

On such a dawn,
The wood was still and silent
Save for a zephyr rustling the leaves,
The trill of the song thrush,
The careful tread of the hiker's boot.
The world rejoiced,
Each burgeoning tree and flower,
Both man and beast,
All sentient life.

The land singed brighter,
Hotter,
As the high-noon sun bathed all in its glow,
Warming, infusing.
One listened close and rapt
As the ash trees waved and whispered,
The crickets sang,
And the verdant meadows,
Dotted with daisy and clover,
Teemed with rabbit in somnolent pursuit of sustenance.

All boundlessly voiced the hymn of the Earth,
The hovering butterfly,
The tending shepherd,
The eagle fowl upon the rise.
They intoned as one
A paean of song,
As approbation to the grace,
The majesty,
The apotheosis that is creation.

12/04/2001

IN EXTREMIS

The agony of loss,
So choked, bereft and numb,
One cannot even weep.
Buried alive in bitter, black despair,
Keening in a silent scream
That swells and ululates enough
To shatter the very oriel of Heaven.

Gruelling ache in every pore,
A crescendo of anguish,
A living death,
A funeral pyre.
Suttee and crucifixion,
Sacrifice and execution,
Butchery and mutilation.

Mute and bitten tongue,
Exsanguinated veins,
Excoriated flesh,
Eviscerated gut,
Shattered, twisted limbs,
Bloodied riven heart,
Arteries furred with pain.

Eyes sightless and inward turned,
Never again to glory in the filigree moon
Or gilded sun,
Or gaze Heavenward to watch the susurrating raindrops,
Now but tears unshed.
And ears that hear not
The call of the living,
Drifting by in a silent stream beyond the glass,
Or even the howling of the wind
As it tears and shreds.

Now standing lone and alone,
In a world gone dark
Without the stars to light the way.

17/01/1998

LABYRINTH OF LUCIDITY

The thoughts so fill my head,
But articulation an ordeal,
Words a convoluted stutter,
An onus to convey,
I fall increasingly silent.

I am losing it,
It ebbs away,
The cognition so prized,
Yet accepted once without question.
I find it now a labour
To concentrate,
Recollect,
Work my way through intricate analysis,
The labyrinth of lucidity.

Vacuity begins to take me over,
Entrenches.
I deliberate,
Where will be the end?
In a final resting place of unmindfulness,
Enmeshed within a maze of diction,
A surreal lexicon I can no longer fathom?

I think of her with sadness,
My dearest, fragile, ancient love,
Engulfed by her confusion,
And ask fearfully,
Who will be the worse in time,
The greater dispossessed.
Lost in another dimension,
The continent of amnesia,
She,
Or I.

27/02/2011

MIRAGE

Cool as white flame,
Sere as the kraal,
Far as an eastern star.

Dry as the wind
That blows the dunes,
Hot as the sun,
Cold as desert night.

Oasis,
Water.
Mirages,
When love is but
A footstep in the sand.

1978

MORTALITY BITES

I wait at the crossroads now,
For mortality begins to bite,
Will render me one of those who are recalled
In a quiet moment,
A figure in a faded photograph,
Of the past,
Not the present,
As was,
Not is.

I am afraid,
Not of the dying,
But the suffering,
The lingering, crippling helplessness.
The nature of the journey to a latter world,
Another state of being,
Poses an enigma,
A conundrum to which there can be no answer,
But perhaps death unbeknownst
Offers sanctuary.

I so weary of it all,
The treadmill of disease,
As the sicknesses multiply,
Consume the body,
Feasting greedily upon the viscera,
Sucking dry the life force.

But one has the choice,
However equivocal,
To be accepting as that endless night encroaches.
Step upon the shadow path with sanguinity,
And find perhaps
Not a stygian darkness,
But rather, the serenity of a phantasmagorical universe
Striated with sunlight,
Iridescent stardust,
Strewn deep and fragrant with spectral blossom.

13/05/2010

PRIERE

O my dear Lord,
Let me reach through the clouds
And see the sun,
Render me not crippled and anguished,
And huddled small
Like a beast in pain.

Restore unto me my promise,
Once so luminescent,
Fierce and bright.
Grant me joy,
That I might dance,
And sing once more
With resounding voice.

Bless me yet
With all that was to be,
But never was.
Let my star ascend to the Heavens,
If only once,
That it might elucidate and shine,
And cast blessed light
On all I hold so dear.

Above all,
Ungrateful though I be,
Hand me reason
To voice thanks
For all upon me
Thou bestowed,
And then denied.

17/09/1997

SANCTUARY

Although not raised within the precincts of the borough,
I feel indigenous now,
Have walked its dusty, vigorous and bustling thoroughfares
a thousand times,
Observed its metamorphosis,
From homogeny,
To melting pot of classes, cultures,
Thronging the rainbow markets,
Lading the shops with custom.

A neighbourhood of contrasts.
Amid the sprawling, monolithic council blocks,
Spread languorously beneath the autumn sun
The aspect is of gabled terraces,
Impeccably preserved,
An affluent oasis,
Tranquil, neat, quiescent.

This constituency most venerable,
Still echoes to the tread of Roman feet
If one visualises trenchantly,
Is the fulcrum for Dickens' penning,
Vivid, vibrant,
Shakespeare's Globe,
His oeuvre a benefaction to the nation.

There are anxieties,
The grief of death and gunfire on the streets,
Poverty and deprivation,
Souls stateless and desperate,
Come to cast themselves upon the grace
Of Southwark for asylum.
Here too,
I, child of refugees of long ago,
Holocaust survivors,
Reside in grateful sanctuary.

2007

SOLACE

I seek only to offer comfort brave knight.
Though seeming fragile be our bond,
It is not fleeting nor as delicate as gossamer,
And would catch you should you fall.
For you dwell deep within my consciousness,
Nestling warm and safe and secret,
And I in yours.

Though you express little of your feelings,
It will suffice,
For I know you through and through,
And with clarity perceive your soul,
Compassionate, tender,
Courageous, modest,
With many a thought unspoken.

So look to yourself stout heart,
As you do too rare,
And,
Though scant you believe,
Place your trust now in God
And in those who care,
Such as I.

12/02/2001

SPINDRIFT

Was it mere spindrift,
Tossed high upon
The meniscus of the seas?
Blown spray,
For an instant opalescent,
Sublime,
A chromatic arc of rainbow,
But now alas,
Long since dulled and pitted
Like tarnish on a silvered plate?

Even if it be,
I might not succumb,
But should instead,
Like a star in the firmament,
Aspire to implode.

And scatter in my wake,
Vistas of such fire,
Charisma,
And joy,
That all who ever crossed my path
Would gasp,
And muse,
And smile with rue.

12/11/1997

THE CHILDREN OF GOD

There are souls on this Earth who turn none away.
They solace the bereaved,
And give of themselves to the poor,
The old,
The sick,
The disturbed,
The frail and weak.
They judge not humanity if they be needy,
Not for them to find the recipients of their charity wanting.

They sit far above us all,
Holding aloft the torch of mercy to light our faltering paths,
Guardians of the World.
They ask for nothing,
Look not to themselves,
Only to the needs of others.
Their compassion is fierce and true,
Their modesty humbling,
The act of giving for them is as the air they breathe.

One day, who knows,
When my wounds be healed,
And my thought at last at peace,
Shall I too be so?
But for this moment
I must stay quiet and still,
And pray for my own salvation.
I fear I shall ever disappoint the generous of heart by my
ungiving,
For truly I can never be as they.

So, for now,
I must instead be but thankful,
Though my own dear Heaven is far out of reach,
That throughout all trauma,
Whenever I have stumbled or failed,
I have been blessed to encounter these children of God,
By them redeemed,
And touched
By the sweet hand of comfort.

01/09/2000

THE GREAT AND THE GOOD

I watch from afar,
The golden ones,
For they cup all the stars in their graceful hands,
Riches, vigour, joyousness, might,
Caskets of treasure,
Jewels from on high,
Patricians legated to inherit the Earth,
With intellect fierce,
Far greater than mine,
The Ubermensch granted the glittering crown.

Do they question their fortune?
For the air of Valhalla they were born fair to breathe,
The great and the good.
With envy I gaze not,
Nor with bitterness seethe,
But rather in wonder.
Perhaps my own slender life
Could, like theirs, be more gilt,
But with less lustre and shine?
For I do not request such existence sublime.

We cannot select our terrestrial fate,
For high in the Heavens our fairway is wrought,
But if one clears the hurdles,
The dice tumble well.
All I ask,
If only,
Dear God,
Were my spirit less frail.

I ask not for more than was writ by design,
But must I strive without hope
From the good Earth to rise?
I beg not for glory,
To Olympus ascend,
To touch not the sun
Nor my knee to unbend,
For these acts without effort such heights to bestride,
Are but gifts that enthrone only glittering lives.

21/05/2002

HERESY

Just a paranoiac
Obsessed with malady,
Subject to delusion,
Hypochondria,
A narcissist with bizarre beliefs,
A public nuisance
One should circumvent.

I crave attention,
Conjure up lurid symptoms of disease,
Seditiously waste the time
Of physicians who ought to bestow their compassion,
Expertise,
Purely upon the deserving unwell,
Dare voice
That obscene expletive,
Allergy.

Deservedly a pariah,
I merit the opprobrium of society
As it rightfully castigates me,
Vents its spleen,
Must bear the mark of Cain,
Dissolving into shadow
Without protestation,

Be not within the world,
In purdah.

Compelled to supplicate in shame,
Ask for less than nothing,
For that is all that should be offered,
Pollute not the air with my heresies,
Present no longer an affront to decency
In my worthlessness,
Deceit.

Abase myself,
Recant,
Beg your forgiveness
On servile knee.

16/05/2015

THE SEVENTIETH SUMMER

We gathered in celebration,
Not ostentatiously,
But with festive, quiet grace.
It lent a comfort,
A profound delight
To be invited to attend
So peerless an occasion.

In later years,
I might reflect
How easily we came together,
To acknowledge,
Pay due homage.

I owed them much,
Almost all I was,
And am,
And shall ever be.

I cast thought upon them now,
So very dear.
Although fragile,
Ageing,
I envisage them undimmed by time,
Still dazzlingly vibrant,
Serenely charismatic,
Hearts beating concomitantly.

20/12/2006

THE SHEPHERD

When we meet,
We shall gather
In quiet remembrance,
To mourn and reflect,
Recollect him
With fondness.

As one,
We might not weep,
Rather,
Restrain our sadness,
But sorrow deeply,
Offer up at his passing
A tacit affection,
Respect for a mentor,
A shepherd who tended us well.

Unforeseen,
He has left us,
His existence cut short.
We must bid him farewell,
From his flock,
An Adieu.

28/04/2005

TO THAT OTHER LIFE BEYOND DEATH

How diminished she seemed,
Weightless,
Swaddled in the crisply, sheeted bed.
Neat,
Eyes tight shut,
She lay almost silent,
Detached,
Neither eating nor drinking,
As she prepared without fuss
To slip away.

Although she was of little worldly consequence,
She was demonstrably loved.
A blithe, untroubled spirit,
She was held in deep affection
By her carers,
United in their sorrow
By her quiet demise.

I believe she felt within her soul
Her time had come,
That it was the hour
To turn her face to the wall,
And depart from the world
Peacefully
And without struggle,
To that other life beyond death.

07/02/2008

WORDLESS

I am still that frightened child,
Selectively mute,
Imprisoned in silence.

I struggle to express my anguish,
But the words will not come.
I listen,
Yet cannot speak.
Too timorous to engage in life with brio,
Or share heartily in your pleasures,
Suffocated by solitude.

I despair at my retrogression.
Appalled,
I note the inexorable advance
Of weakness, age,
Loss of cognition,
The self as it shatters,
Falls away shard by shard.

You regard me with incomprehension,
Disinterest,
Turn away,
Not intentionally unkind,
Just baffled,
Alienated,
Touched with mild distaste at my oddness.

I acquiesce in the unequal conflict
With the viscous, wordless mire
That consumes me,
Fractionates my being.
However much you care,
And some still do,
You might yet cast me
Merely a perfunctory lifeline.

Too late,
For I am beyond rescue now,
Adrift,
Too far out for salvation.

15/04/2009

THIRD AGE

Still comprehending,
Doughty, stoic, kind,
With wit and humour not entirely fled,
Now shuttered in dementia,
With past bereavements
Almost lain to rest.
The hope,
Excised,
Released,
As grieving memories,
Painful trauma fades.

Might Eva sit at peace,
Serene,
Her sorrowed thought
A blanket of forgetfulness,
To spend her days
In comfort and repose,
No more in want of shelter,
Warmth,
Nor care.

Her milky eyes,
Lit bright by Kosher feasts,
Of solace, cheer and pleasure
To her now,
Her wretched, swollen hand,
Frail and faltering,
Takes grateful hold as nourishment abounds.
Food, the staff of life,
Now buoys her dogged,
Sparrow frame.

Though chutzpah,
Spark and spirit
Now be almost past,
Still swells the heart
To see her safe and clean,
No longer sad, sequestered,
Locked in fear,
With pain of lonely isolation healed.
And young again,
Not eighty-one,
But thirty-six she dreams.

1999

STONE UPON THE GRAVE

Never might I stand
At their graveside,
Nor place a stone
Upon their resting place,
For I know not who they were,
Or how they perished,
Or where or if they lie.

Had they endured,
I should have been apprised
Of their story,
But they passed away
Amid an opacity
Of unutterable horror,
Denied elemental deliverance.

The time is too long fled
To undertake the lacerating journey
To the camps of death,
In endeavour to offer reparation,
Vast and merciless cemeteries
Where no birds sing,
Soil upon which perhaps
They were set to ash,
And drifted to Heaven,
Blameless.

Too late now
To disclose their narratives,
For no survivors are there left alive
To tell their fate,
Their own life on Earth curtailed now,
And gone in silence
Keeping their counsel.

16/06/2014

THE SUN WILL RISE TOMORROW

When I anguish to excess,
Commit anxieties to paper
In endless, desultory lines,
Streams of utter misery,
You chide me a little,
Decline to peruse the writings
Of excoriating rhyme,
And say gently,
The sun will rise tomorrow,
And I smile.

We have been matched
An eon,
Soul to soul,
Sharing our affections,
Trauma,
Stark concerns
In reciprocated empathy,
Turning absolutely to the other
For buttered solace and loving kindnesses.

But will come the time
To say farewell
Through sheer, sad circumstance,
Determine it no longer feasible
To walk in synchronicity?
Accept we cannot with effect
Extend a steely hand
To ease the other's tribulations?

Be not here a lifetime
If needs be,
To offer remedy?
And might my grief be unrelenting
In the face of such grinding loss,
And my tears run deep
As the rivers of Babylon?
Or shall I smile
And watch the sunrise?

08/02/2012

HOLOCAUST

I flinch on catching footage of them,
Huddled,
Circumscribed behind the ravening barbed wire,
Skeletal,
Starving,
In filthy rags,
Gazing through the rusted bars
Without hope or emotion.

Those depicted
Were perhaps my kin.
They died in a manner so iniquitous,
There are simply no words
To articulate its bestiality.
Survivors from within my family
Erected a wall of silence,
A turning away from their trauma,
Aching only to forget,
No mention of their experiences,
Or naming of the lost.

Those exterminated were of my ancestry,
Race,
But I was spared,
Born after the atrocities were halted,
Although there will never come an end
In the grieving hearts
Of those of us
Who were not erased,
And we have an obligation to remember,
And mourn.

I cannot call up their pain
Without dissolving in my own sadness,
Or lay to rest their spirits,
Nor resurrect their image,
For their faces are mired
Forever in shadow.

So be it,
The ochred past and its terrors,
Their agony,
Never to be dismissed nor forgotten
As long as we,
Their descendents draw breath.
They are long deceased now,
But perhaps their souls still repose
In that no man's land
Between death and life,
In neither dignity
Nor peace.
I pray it be other.

29/02/2012

HEARTH

My home is as peerless
As verse sublime,
The most fragrant flower,
The tenderest song,
Humming with shimmering colour,
Poppy,
Flame,
Buttercup,
Mink,
Shades elemental,
Symbols of life.

A child of deprivation,
Although never in utter want,
I yearned to realise
Within the chasm of my soul,
The fantasy of the cushioned womb,
A dwelling exquisite,
Neat,
Secure.

As I matured,
I embraced yet fiercer
This secret longing
For the sanctuary
I had never known.
I cast extravagant imaginings
Ever more elaborate
Of my desert island haven.
The curtains I would stitch,
The jewelled carpets spin,
The furniture fine construct.
Nail wood to the roof,
Cosy and enclosing.

And so I assembled my eyrie,
Tucked away at the peak of the world,
Envisaged,
Accomplished,
Twig by twig.
In response,
In hour of trauma
Or defeat,
It offers succour,
For it sings to me a lullaby of peace,
A sanctum for desolate times.

So as I gaze at its perfection,
At each vase,
Picture,
Artefact in its tidy place,
Its vibrant
Tranquil stillness,
I am comforted,
For whatever befalls me,
It will shelter and cocoon,
And enfold me tight
Within its glowing heart.

It holds the essence of my spirit,
For we are one,
Mother and child,
Parent and daughter,
Entwined together in loving symbiosis.

13/07/2000

JOURNEY WITHOUT END

Shall I sink no lower.
I now feel little but futility,
An apathy of non-being,
A lack of hope,
Of life,
A dimming of the soul.

Despair would be too sentient a word,
For within sits only void,
A numbness of spirit,
Inexpressible,
Deep-buried anguish that I can no longer touch.

Are you out there anyone,
Near enough to take my hand
And guide me safe
Into the light?

I fear you hear too faint,
For my voice is falling silent,
Choking in the echoing miasma
That surrounds me.
My tongue is stilled,
Unable to call.

Perhaps,
One day,
I shall emerge from my chilling oubliette
And behold the sun,
But who knows?
I have scant faith in my redemption,
And feel utterly alone,
Hearken only from afar
Response to my voiceless prayer.

Shall I someday find the answer,
And be exultant,
Or do I travail for nothing,
Travel unceasing.
Condemned to walk forever blind
Through the darkness of midnight,
In solitude,
And without purpose?

12/02/2001

IN SPIRIT

I watched their kin
With affection,
Familially seated
At the Seder repast,
Here was convened their legacy.
Absent,
Yet still with us,
Recalled
And cherished.

We reclined in comfort,
To the left as ordained,
With ease,
Acknowledging with ritual
Biblical times,
Shared history,
When the Israelites fled Egypt,
Manumitted from bondage.

The great-grandchildren,
Engaging offspring,
Tall and rosy,
Vigorous,
Healthy, clever,
Joshing each other
With exuberant kindliness,
The youngest infant
Passed adoringly
From arm to arm.

Powerful was the presence
Of their progenitors
On this unutterably holy day,
Their charisma and sanctity
Still manifest
In the glory of their descendants.

I felt blessed
To be present,
To be invited to share
This hallowed occasion,
And again reflected,
Eyes moistening a little,
For they were still amid us
In spirit,
Had never left.

21/06/2012

AMIGO

As once he was,
In sublime foregone years
Of azure skies
And blithe contentment,
So shall we remember him,
Recall his mischievous innocence,
Exuberance.

We mourn his death together,
With implicit sadness.
He was one of us,
A fraternity of colleagues
Conjoined over time,
A cohort now the poorer
For his absence.

He rests now,
No longer striving
To sustain the burden
Life anchored upon him.
No more anguish,
Amigo,
Adios,
Sleep well.

11/09/2012

OBSESSION

As I listen
To the endless thrumming
Seeping through the floor
Almost twenty four seven,
I feel
I am descending almost into lunacy.

It rarely ceases,
The expression of what I perceive
As his addiction,
Compulsion to play music remorselessly,
Ad infinitum,
His ruthless, driven singlemindedness
Chilling.
He cannot tear himself away
From what he calls
His very life,
Considers his unendurable behaviour
Unimpeachable.

Almost all have turned away,
Irritated,
Bored,
Indifferent.
I have been counselled to move,
Castigated for desperately,
Pathetically,
Taking a stand
Against him
And his intimidating tribe.

It is utterly intolerable,
Lying awake in the early hours
Of the morning,
Compelled to listen
To a marathon of drumbeats,
Rising,
Rising,
Nerves stretched like piano wire,
Aching for sleep.

I cannot accept
The ordeal will never arrest,
Still unrealistically envisage a time
There will come an end
To such insanity.
Have pity you world,
Out there,
Do not condemn me
To a life disquieted
By this cacophonous obsession.

08/08/12

CHIMERA

On tranquil days she sleeps within,
Is barely present,
Fleeting,
Like a dreamless thought just drifting out of reach,
But commonly,
Sits hard and mordant,
Solid, indestructible as lava stone.
I cannot tell you of her form,
For she has many, as does the chimera,
To outwit the few who seek her.
She is misted in obfuscation,
Floats ethereal and ghostly, though is also rabid.
She does exist in truth in terms of physiology,
But invisible, the haunting of a poltergeist.

But perennially, I feel her weighty, pressing,
As a dark and scaly monster buried deep,
Although an amorphous spectre is that other self,
The incubus, my alter ego.
Still I am uncertain of what she wills and intends,
Likes and abhors,
For the list is endless,

But if gainsaid, she punishes with vigour.
My body and my intellect enchained,
Enmeshed in her thrall,
Bow to her every wish,
For her omnipotence is absolute.

Far beyond comprehension she lies,
For it imposes a labour intractable to disentangle
her matrix,
Within from without,
And as for me, as with few other,
The mind is the body, and the body the mind,
And cannot be rent asunder.

Although you would have I am mad,
I observe this formless being as though there were
two of us,
I the host,
And she the alien,
The unwelcome guest who will never leave.
She does not watch me watching,
But is all consciousness,
Demanding as an ailing infant who must be succoured,
Wordless yet undeniable.

All of my life she has lain in wait and dormant,
And when her time did come,
Awakened and made fully known her presence,
Fearful and razor-sharp,
Her intangible yet hegemonic power.
That she has to be acknowledged is all I know,
What was, and is, and will ever be,
Together and forever we bond,
One spirit, one corpus, and one soul.

10/11/2012

CHILD OF THE INSTITUTION

Once upon a time,
There did shine a star of rainbow hue,
Or perhaps a flower of some delicacy
That did bloom in arid soil.
A lonely child in a parentless land.

And this tiny star did radiate ever brighter and bolder,
Rising ever higher in her little firmament.
She sang with beguiling voice,
A solo soprano in the synagogue choir.
Ever busy,
She stitched and sewed and knitted.
Clothes and shoes for herself,
Outfits for her dolls,
And fancy dress costumes of such design
That none other could compare.

She built and created.
With no home to call her own,
She pasted cottages out of paper with longing,
Sculptured pets out of Sabbath candle wax,
Fashioned toys for her playmates.
She devised games for them too.
One year, a Summer Fair with great ingenuity
And fun.

A clever thespian,
Funny, bossy and bold,
With crystal tones,
A storyteller of invention.
Every night as she lay in bed,
Did her companions plead for her to relate them
just one tale.
"Too tired!" would say she,
"Then two tomorrow!" they would cry,
And so she did,
Spinning fantasies for them as they lay abed
listening.

She dwelt in this other universe,
One of fantasy and imaginings,
Cut off from the outside world,
Under the ocean asleep,
Protected by her slumber.
Books too were her life,
Of every genre.
Always deaf to all,
Buried in words,
Ever reading and writing.

A dynamo within,
Fizzing and humming,
Bursting with life-force and energy.
Too much of everything,
Too much of nothing at all.

So there came an end,
So it did,
When she departed from the arid but sheltered land
In which childhood had passed,
When the candle burned lower.
For so brief a time
It had flamed so bright.
Lower and lower,
And then,
Snuffed out, burnt out.

The little star had ceased to shine
Without whatever is the stuff of life,
Love, home, family,
Sense of self,
Sense of worth,
Sense of being.
In the end,
Displaced,
So crippled,
So stunted by fear of the world outside,
The child, Then the woman, Just ceased to be.

29/11/98

NEPAL

From afar
They chartered in
To perform in concert.
Gladly they had offered their time,
Deities of their elected instruments,
Drawn together on this day
With unique intent.

A hushed murmur
In the audience,
Well educated,
Well bred,
Habitués of these occasions.
Within the graceful church
And its acoustics of perfection,
The pews gradually filled
With such heartfelt devotees
Ready to give,
Partake of the evening's cornucopia.

What were my expectations?
I am not entirely sure,
Not a regular participant at such functions,
But I became aware
Of the privilege of the circumstance

Of simply being there.
So singular an experience,
In so close a proximity to the orchestra,
Quite remarkable,
Not a little disconcerting perhaps
Sat almost eye to eye,
And paying so little to be present.

The musicians gathered
By the vestry door,
Exquisitely attired,
Coiffed,
Beautiful in their talent
With strong, clever faces,
Traversing to their seats.
Then, addressing us,
The celebrity presenter,
At length
To foster our philanthropy,
And introducing,
Schmoozing the performers
And their iconic, charismatic,
Venerable conductor.

And so they began to play.
The music soared
With such a power
One was uplifted almost
From one's seat with astonishment

And pleasure,
Such glory,
The best of the best.
They performed together
With a pure familiarity,
A great family come together again
Playing into the twilight.

Magical it was,
And we met there
Honoured to do so,
Intimate a sharing
Of so rare an evening,
An experience not to be forgotten,
Stored away preciously within the mind,
To be taken out,
Polished and reflected upon
In a later,
Quietly euphoric instance.

02/06/2015

A poem dedicated to the occasion of the concert held at St. James, Piccadilly, on 28 May 2015, in aid of the disaster in Nepal, performed by former members of the Academy of St. Martin-in-the-Fields, conducted by Sir Neville Marriner, and introduced by John Suchet.

ISN'T ONE AFFLICTION ENOUGH?

I bear no rancour,
Although blighted
By multiple sickness,
Polio,
Mental illness,
And now,
Allergy of both body and mind.
Accidents of nature.
I blame none,
Not He,
Nor my fellow man,
It's just the roll of the dice.
After all, I've survived.

If I were of little faith,
I should reproach Him on high for a cruel joke,
Isn't one affliction enough?
Why was I selected to ail with triple ferocity?
Be fair,
Portion it out I would say,
Allow others their slice of suffering,
I'm sure they'd express deep gratitude.

I'm neither sour nor angry,
Why should I be?
Everything's peachy,
So I shouldn't complain,
People don't like it.
Be stoical like Job,
Behave myself,
Stiff upper lip and all that.
And it's my fault anyway I'm pressed to believe,
All of my own making.
Hysterical neurosis, delusion, obsession,
Yet another figment of my overheated imagination.
They listen but hear nothing,
Don't perceive I'm not waving but drowning.

Allow me at least to feel bewildered, dazed,
Numb with disbelief at such bizarre disorder,
Multiple Allergy.
The Coup de grace.
I'm a Universal Reactor,
Or rather nuclear reactor, Jack teased.
Don't they say that there are more things under
the sun…?

My body just finds things obnoxious,
Not at all to its taste,
Too fastidious by half.
Quite understandable.
No liking for creams, lotions, chemicals,
Innocuous pollutants,
Even stripy toothpaste,
Just the humdrum currency of quotidian life for others,
But for my physiology, gravely toxic.

As for my brain,
Well!
A comforting beverage or cigarette are entirely out
of the question,
Since they drive my cerebrum into absolute frenzy,
To the edge of insanity,
Towering mania.
Even noise, people, books, emotion, thought,
Medicines, pain, it cannot withstand.

And humble wheat,
(And what else does it hate?
I'll have to investigate.
Then again, why bother to eat at all?)
Humble wheat, harboured,
Hidden in scrumptious pastries, bread, pasta, biscuits,
chocolate,
Even homely pickle.
Their tastes will just have to fade into memory,
As no more must they pass my lips
For fear my pernickety brain is offended, cross,
Upset at the intrusion of such foreign matter,
And contracts into pulsing tightness.

And convulses,
Is crushed in an invisible vice-like grip,
Boils over,
Explodes in feverish phobic thought.
And I am overcome by panic, fear, paranoia, despair,
Utterly alone in my pain,
Devoured by it as others look on unseeing.

And I itch from head to toe,
My scalp crawls as if laden with lice,
I can barely draw breath,
My hair falls out by the handful,
My jaw grinds,
I obsessively ache to shake, stamp and rock,
My gut becomes bloated and raw,
And my muscles turn rigid and clench
As with tension they crack.

And ever, ever,
If without puissant drugs,
(Enough to fell a horse),
Sleepless are the long nights,
And every molecule of my being is eviscerated by
crucifying exhaustion.

Polio,
(The viral cause of this sickness?)
Rather pales by comparison,
Doesn't it?
A minor ailment almost,
Nothing to worry one,
So dwarfed is it by the monstrousness,
The abomination that is allergy.

Just a bad dream.
Something I ate or drank perhaps?
So, I'll sleep tonight,
And wake tomorrow to a bright dawn,
And the nightmare will have fled into the darkness,
And I'll be hearty and sane and well again,
Just like you.

30/03/2000

LAND OF THE SUN

To bask in the sunshine,
Not root in the dark,
To be bathed in warmth and health and love.
To be encompassed within the cloak of belonging,
Being of, not apart.
To be joyous,
To be well,
To be strong,
To be whole,
To be not sinister, but right.

On this great planet Earth,
Gaia,
There dwell two peoples,
Those who have all,
And those with nought,
And the wall between them is glassy and high
and barbed,
And one I could never scale to the land of the sun,
Try as I might.
And I did,
So very hard,
All of my life.

And my world being one of illusion,
And being unsound in body and mind,
I clung always to this barrier with hands uneasy
and trembling,
Balanced with shaking stance,
Poised,
Ready to slip one side or other.

But being not meek,
I did not inherit this earth,
And there was no soul to break my fall.

So I stumbled into the shadows,
Into the twilight world of the wanting,
The workless,
The despised,
The sick,
The mad,
The undeserving,
The forgotten.

But now, at last,
Can I rest, let go?
Take time to ease the pain of life in reclusion,
And reflect upon the path that lies ahead?
It is one of shards and weeds,
Uneven and rocky,
But even pebbles have lustre,
And flowers of the wild
Colour and scent.

06/02/1999

THE DARK PLACE

You will always be there,
The dark place,
Burrowed deep,
Perched on my soul like a hooded crow.
I cannot deny your power,
Nor watch you unfearing with my inner eye,
For you are the stuff of night,
Weighty, black and crushing.

We have grown together,
Have we not?
Lifelong, we have dwelt uneasily as one,
You part of me, and I of you.
I have passed my days in your umbra,
Rendered by its darkness crippled, sere.
From you binding shackle I cannot shake free,
Though I strain so hard to rise,
For I am a flightless, grounded bird.

I have followed the path to maturity,
But still she kneels in pain within the dark place,
That sickly, weeping infant, my alter ego,
Bent and burdened.
She cries to the world, if only it would hear,
And cannot be soothed.
Never will she spread her wings,
It is far too late for manumission now.

So to live my life,
However long or brief my stay,
I must endeavour to reach acceptance of a kind,
A coming to terms with the sad child in the dark place,
For whatever befalls,
She will be my companion from first to last.
With almighty strength,
I must not reject her,
Nor cast upon her blame for what was not to be,
Spit neither hate nor anger,
Offer hope, compassion, love
And so for myself, grant absolution.

I can never set her free,
So I must allow that she curls piteously tight
Within that dark place,
For good or ill forever,
And will accompany me on the last long journey
To God and eternity.

16/03/2002

SONG FOR RAPHAEL

I did not know you well
Cousin Raphael.
Never glimpsed your face
Nor shook your hand.
You were ever but the disembodied voice
Of a sick man
Of great age,
Distantly-related kin
At the end of a telephone line
So far away.

But your intonation was intrinsic
As the beating of my heart.
A race memory,
The enchanting accent of old Vienna,
So clear, unmistakable,
The song of my ancestry,
My blood,
My family,
My far-distant roots.

Although we never met,
And I knew little of your past,
Your courage,
Just the bare bones of your history in anecdote,
When Esther Rosen read to me
Your cousin Henry's brief but moving entry
In the Jewish Chronicle,
I felt shaken,
Grieved by all the horror that befell you
In your long traumatic life.

And filled with a sad pride
For the cousin I barely knew.
You I shall not forget in your passing.
It is not too late to light the candle in Memoriam,
Though already lain at peace as you wished
In the manner of your much-mourned parents,
They in atrocity cremated,
You set to ash in remembrance.

To the end of your life,
You fought so hard
To right their wrongs.

Written in memory of cousin Raphael Wand. His parents died in
Minsk Concentration Camp, and subsequently he became
Political Interrogator of German Field Marshal Keitel at the
Nuremberg War Trials in 1945.

25/02/2001

NO REFLECTION IN THE GLASS

I am other,
Set apart from the norm
Of Homo Sapiens,
A timorous soul,
Ill-equipped,
Lacking the emotional bulwark
Inimitable to survival.

My spirit adheres to pain,
Is an attractant for trauma.
I creak heavily with neurosis,
Am laden with paranoia,
Regarded by they who care not to know me
With neither interest
Nor charity.

I am afeared of those
Unheedingly cruel, sharp beings,
Their icy judgement snaps my bones.
I perceive myself to be insignificant,
Amorphous,
Yet still I might with melancholy
Grieve the loss,
Should my creative essence
Diminish.

But despite the fire of invention
Steaming within
To validate my existence,
I flounder,
Am cloaked in invisibility,
Cast no reflection in the glass.

20/07/2013

IN MEMORIAM

My father stood in witness
To the slaughter of his kindred.
Genocide,
Execution,
The final solution.
The guns were raised,
The barrels steadied,
The shots fired.
How many bullets did it take to kill the Juden?

Then the interment.
No Kaddish for his brothers,
No prayer for the dead as the swastikas looked on,
And compelled him to dig their graves.
And in his grief,
He rose up,
And for his anguish,
They seized and hung him.
They bound together his feet, and from a branch he swung,
Suspended, inverted.

Forgive me, forgive me my father,
I was nought but a child,
Unknowing,
I did not share your pain,
Could feel only coldness and dread
At your poor tortured madness,
Your psychosis of fear,
Your insanity of suffering.

August 1997

LEFT NOTHING TO REGRET

I watch them as she comforts him
With empathetic tenderness.
They share an elegant, gentle, understated love,
An ageless, symbiotic partnership.

Both racked by pain,
They move with the care and unsteadiness of
extreme old age,
Infirmity.
Hampered, yet stoic,
Never a real bitterness is voiced,
Just his occasional, exhausted, plaintive wish
To be free of his discomfort.

I visit them on occasion,
Am privileged to be permitted to share their time
As they slowly approach the final chapter.
In all the years they have passed together,
So long and fittingly,
They have wasted not a moment,
Left nothing to regret.

Watched over heedfully by their caring,
Ebullient, glorious clan,
They sit with great dignity,
Acceptance,
Her quiet, attentive presence at his side
A soothing emollient for his anguish.
Still so lucid, sage and humorous,
She takes all in her stride.

So very long ago,
She merited the right to take her ease,
Yet,
Impelled by indomitable, charitable impulse,
And a deeply loving heart,
She seldom rests.
As throughout her lengthy, dutiful,
Immensely fruitful life,
She leaves nought in her world that needs tending,
Untouched.

05/09/2007

QUARANTINE

There coalesces a grief
Within the heart of me now,
A melancholy,
I no longer nurse the illusion,
Aspiration, that I am worthy,
Do not figure in your pantheon
Of esteemed souls,
If ever I did.

Inclined to dissipate,
Meld into that frigid, isolating place
I now occupy,
Hollowed out,
Gutted,
An empty carapace,
Echoing only with racking silence.

One by one
You walked away,
Finding me unwholesome,
Enchanting you only superficially
With my verse
Although I ached for your approbation,
But the moment I displeased you
You sat in judgement,

Conditional compassion withdrawn,
Solace no more on offer.

I failed utterly
To secure your acceptance,
Psychologically diseased
And untouchable as I am,
To be quarantined
With urgency,
Lest I infect you.

06/07/2015

WHO ARE YOU?

Grayson Perry,
Perhaps his alter ego
Informs his art,
Consciousness,
Flamboyance,
The aura he casts,
The rumbustious joyousness
He mines from existence.

His essence is one of eccentric decency,
A merry heart,
Unique perspective on the world,
The verities he poses
Are leavened with lightness,
Easy articulacy,
An unsullied honesty.

A maverick
And a rare, wise man,
One who draws others to him,
Palliated by his understanding
Of their worth,
Their significance illustrated,
Alighted upon with insight
Within his artist eye.

A cadeau of a being,
His work fashioned
Like rainbow, brilliant diadems
That stun us with their virtuosity,
Drawing us in with enchantment
And shock,
The elemental bedrocks
Of his otherworldly moral sentience.

29/11/2014

ASPIRATION

A wish to be born again without pain or fear,
To be strong and free,
For a late flowering,
A reverie of a bursting into bloom
like the rose of an Indian summer,
And a mind of such power and strength
and glitter.
It would shine and shimmer,
It would dance,
It would scorch and burn.

And deep inside is a crystal.
It lies hidden,
Slumbering and still in the dark dank mire
of unconsciousness,
Bound and silent.
Set it free.
Let it spin,
Let its rainbow be cast
So that all who might see it
Would sing,
And marvel,
And find warmth in the shining facets of its prism.

And I should love,
And fill the air with fire
And joy and heat and passion,
And everything I touched
Would glow and grow and blossom.
And my tears would water the seed
To grow strong and green in silent paean.

02/06/1997

SLEIGHT OF HAND

Amanuensis with peerless skills,
Literacy effortless,
Vocabulary,
Syntax sublime.

Could one match elsewhere
Her adroitness,
Her transposition of poem
From scrawl,
To computer,
To copy so seamlessly done?

I write,
She prestidigitates,
By sleight of hand
Transcribes the verse impeccably,
Marshalling each line
With unerring correctness.

Enfin,
With my body of work
To be arrayed in the public domain,
Critiqued,
Censured perhaps,
Attribution is due
To the Eminence Grise,
Transmuter of words,
Of my oeuvre,
The matrix.

02/06/2012

TINNITUS

I used to hear the verse,
As yet unwritten,
Hushed,
Pedantic,
Sonorous,
But now
With insidious stealth
Predates cacophony.

It muddies thought,
Exhausts,
Inducing simultaneously
A degree of deafness
And a muffled crescendo.

Contemplation is turbid,
No turning words
Over and over in the mind
In concentrated silence,
Nor scrutinising each one
For fitness for purpose
With a lucid calm.

I composed with effort,
But on occasion,
Contrapuntally,
The rhyme would trickle out,
Easing like a flowing rivulet,
The poem not perfect,
But a beginning to the narrative
I wished to spin.

I required a pregnant stillness
To write,
The inchoate phrases
Waiting to be born
Quietly expectant,
Before ascending the taut edifice
Upon which I structured inspiration.

I scribe uneasily now
Without that necessary backdrop
Of icy, cutting soundlessness,
Yet pleasing rhythm,
Within my consciousness.

20/05/2012

EPIPHANY

Perhaps a feathered angel kiss,
Epiphany,
The blessing of a child,
Unfurling of a dewy bloom
That lifts its calyx to the light
And is within the world.
Each breath a consecration,
A being fashioned in the image of her God,
Stardust formed and gently perfect,
An innocent with astral soul.

The advent of a new-born life
Begets a tenderness,
Quiescent stirs the epicentre of a lilting universe,
Harmonising lullabies of silvered song
As the infant drifts in slumber,
A continuum of humanity,
Of hope and of divinity.

The gilded dynasty bequeathed
Another generation,
A scion gift with silken bond
Secured toward posterity,
As will become,
And back into a past writ cuneiform.
Her birth, a dazzle of creation,
A lambent palimpsest of God,
His testament of affirmation.

19/03/2005

MUTTERLIEBE

An empty doorway,
She cast not even shadow,
Just a ghost,
An absence of being.
My mother,
Long swallowed up by the midnight past.

In such unendurable pain,
With cancer riddled from brain to breast,
Just thirty four,
So pitifully young.
One still cannot contemplate such agony
Without anguish of one's own.

A darkened room with curtains drawn,
Peas forked into my listless mouth by an invisible
presence,
Four years of age
And already a child alone.

On the day she departed this life,
For supper was served boiled fish and tinned
tomatoes.
With painful bewilderment
I told my fellow orphans of my loss,
And they laughed with indifference
And continued to eat,
But I understood my bereavement no more than they,
So I cannot condemn them,
It was all so long ago.

And thereafter,
Throughout all my childhood years,
As I lay in the dormitory between starchy sheets,
I would suck my thumb,
And weep for my absent parent,
The one I never knew,
Had no memory of,
And stretch out my hand for comfort
From the mother who never came.

GHOST OF A LOVE

Was it really so frail,
The mere ghost of a love,
Was so fragile the link,
Just a sigh on the wind.
So strong was the bond,
Hard as fine-tempered steel,
Yet he melted away like a wraith in the night,
Gone to ground in his pain.

Always I felt him to be but a dream,
An enigma,
Never mine,
There and yet absent,
A gossamer cobweb so light and so fine,
I could brush him away with the touch of a hand.
But I cherished his soul,
My beautiful, magical, valiant man.

But was it ever to be,
For so gentle his psyche,
So tender and lost,
Was it crushed by the weight of a trauma too vast.
A shattered spine,
A broken reed?

The pity, the anguish, the heartache,
The grief of it all.
Must I now mourn him?
I struggled hard not to allow him to fall,
To haul him back from the brink,
To salvage what little was left of his life.
But his vessel I fear her mooring has cast,
And has sailed far away to the land of the lost,
Now shrouded forever in mist of the past.

20/02/2002

COUSIN

On occasion,
I hear an asperity
In his voice
As we talk on the telephone,
A conversation driven by duty
I conjecture.
Perhaps he feels it a mitzvah to call,
Familial obligation,
But he has doubtless
An affection for me,
As I do for him.

I value his kindness,
For this,
A necessary communication,
Perhaps to ensure
That I am still compos mentis,
And not in bother,
For my life is eventful,
Even if only
In a somewhat meaningless way.

He sits infinitely above me
In the matter of class,
He very much of the upper,
I the lower,
And I feel unequivocally
His inferior
In intellect,
Breeding,
Aptitude,
In fact
In almost everything,
And witter on nervously
When we converse.

He has a good heart,
Sense of humour,
But is at times
Understandably a tad impatient,
Non-committal
Whenever I trot out some bon mot
Of particular witlessness,
Or call at an inconvenient hour,
But he is essentially
All the kin I have,
And I,
The indigent, supplicant relation,
Am sentient
Of his compassion.

17/07/2012

CELEBRATED LIFE

I caught him
On the radio last night,
Clive James,
On a late night talk show.
I was aware he was terminally ill,
Mourned afresh,
Near bursting with sorrow
As on his imminent death
He reflected.

He reminisced about his childhood,
An easy, fun, Aussie start in life,
Too late and difficult now
To return home to say goodbye,
And of all the things he had done
With his time on Earth,
Had intended to do,
And now never would.

Of his glittering achievements,
The TV and journalistic celebrity
Which he had immensely enjoyed,
Talked of it all
In his sanguine, witty,
Omniscient, downbeat way.

He had few profound regrets,
Nor real fears of dying
As he neared the end,
Did not believe in an afterlife,
Held that mortality is only part of living,
And despite leukaemia and emphysema,
Asserted he suffered no pain,
Fortunate,
Unlike others,
And still he treasured the joys
His family continued to bring him.
Even the likelihood of impending blindness
He regarded with equanimity.

Writing,
His foremost talent,
He spoke of with fondness,
His love of the word in all its forms,
And read out a poem
From possibly his final work,
A moving piece,
Valedictory.

As I listened to him
Articulate in his measured Australian twang
His delight in all the world,
Expressing an appreciation
Of the wondrous places on the planet
Upon which he had set foot

In his fulfilling,
If abbreviated existence,
I tried and failed to contain my sadness
For the absence to come
Of the man who had penned
The most hilariously entertaining memoirs
I had ever read,
Still smiling in recall
At the thought of them.

Still the tears fall
As I grieve,
In eulogy,
Will course again
When he is gone.

18/04/2015

POLIO EPIDEMIC

It is of little consequence,
The crippled limb,
The Damocletian sword,
Hovering, haunting
From life unto death,
The only companion of constancy.

The crooked foot,
Reptilian, webbed, askew,
Yet almost fair to look upon,
Dainty, pointed, a dancer's toes.
Of muscle be there little in the calf,
Atrophied, wasted, neat, short,
A rocking gait.

Then the ankle, the fulcrum,
And the fear of further pain and deformity
They say will come with creeping age,
As it wears too thin in the bone.
Already fallen, rolling, flat of arch.
Dislocation of the knee-cap,
Twice over already so,
And certain yet again.
Waits every sliding surface a peril to its stability.

The cold.
With every passing winter season comes the frozen shank,
And the muscles rigid, numb,
The chilblains red and raw.
Each step an icy threat,
All it takes, a skidding fall.

And of the beginning, so very long ago.
The infant, the child of two,
Lain in cot of glass,
Barriered from all comfort.
In paralysis, untouchable.
No soul to soothe away the pain,
The cries, the shedded tears,
The ache of isolation.

The growing years.
The solitary child,
Shackled, fettered, in iron strapped
And wheeled to school.
No liberation,
No striding to freedom like other children.

The catalogue of surgery,
The pain of each procedure,
Five to date, and surely more to come.
In childhood convalescence,
Lying alone in bed,
Dreaming, gazing at the clouds, the sky.
Always so alone.
All my life,
Set alone with my damaged child.

19/07/1998

REQUIEM

With angst still I mourn in bereavement,
On unearthing triste, faded mementoes,
Ghostly echoes of her once so incandescent light,
And of her passing.
You could not know of the love,
Of the bond so strong,
That when she departed it rent out my heart.
So dark and mordant was the grief,
She never wholly slipped away,
So yet she haunts.

She lies now asleep,
Curled, I know not where,
Nor do I wish to,
Quiet, somewhere upon the brow of a rolling, grassy hill,
Watching in peace the sun ascend and the moon aglitter,
Purring mutely in her terrestrial grave.

Might that her suffering were more benign.
In recall, still the pain racks,
For so great was my sorrow.
We were two loving beings bonded as one,
But close to the end she was so light and fragile,
Insubstantial, weightless as a spectre,
Transparent in her sickness.

So heavily weighted the anguish
After my starchild stole away,
Never again shall I have such as she,
For so imprisoned was her soul,
Far above the Earth,
So shuttered within,
She was denied the inalienable right of her breed under
God's Heaven,
To roam as she willed,
To predate and explore.
So trapped and penned was her spirit,
With her very essence she ached to be free.

So at last I hope,
As quiet you rest in slumber eternal my love,
That you ache no more,
And in absolution for caging your soul,
I release to the stars a gossamer wish,
A spinning dove to carry my prayer.
As in life were your dreams,
You now run free with the wind.

08/07/2002

IN HIS ABSENCE

Ere the moon
Quiescent fall,
Bank the flame
Lest passion die,
Pray my love will not forget me,
Touch with dew his sylvan eyes.

Shield his star
And lend him succour,
His spirit render cruel and brave,
Gird his strength
To course and vanquish,
Swaddled warm
And wrapt with love.

If be long ere
I should see him,
Cast Thy cloak around his soul,
Twine his heart
With threads of sunlight,
Guard his tender psyche well.

So until that evidential day,
Hold him fierce
And tend him still,
Unto Thee I hand his keeping,
Cherish dear
If be Thy will.

A MOURNING

I shall think of them as one
As she is carried to her final resting place,
Side by side,
In death immutable,
Indivisible,
Reunited in that life beyond life.

It will be a funeral of solemnity
But a great occasion,
An impassioned tribute
To an extraordinary,
Profoundly gifted,
Righteous, graceful soul.
The world is infinitely the poorer
For her passing.

Many tears will be shed.
I shall offer up my sorrow
In the midst of a gathering
Of her prodigious,
Multitudinous kin.
I too shall pray for her spirit,
That it might slumber at peace in Eternity,
Give thanks
That I was bestowed such a blessing
In the knowing of her.

So now,
Together they will rest at last,
An end to suffering,
Utter tranquillity,
Their journey done,
Complete in their perfect, immeasurable love.
In death,
As in life.

07/11/2011

A VISCERAL FRAGILITY

I hesitate,
Devoured by visceral fragility.
Enervated, spiritless,
Drained of essence,
As though dispersing into shadow,
I hover without purpose,
In want of dignity.

Psychologically disquieted,
I drift along upon a tide of melancholia,
Fretting,
Sustained only by a futile optimism
That all will be well
If I pay no regard to my frailty,
Deny the undeniable.

If I spirit away into atom,

Will you note my disembodiment,

Grieve at my non-being,

Ache a little for that which once I was?

Or will you sigh briefly,

Regretfully,

But with a slight impatience,

Then turn aside with succinct deliberation,

And move on with your life?

06/09/2006

REFLECTION

Cousin Adolf,
I perceive you through the prism of the blood-red past,
But you did not leave without remembrance,
For still your verse springs strong and ringing from the page,
Testament to the endurance of the human soul.
I stand deep in your shadow,
Cast darkly,
And never will my pen flow fine or fierce as yours,
Or be as feted or revered,
But it matters little.

In honesty, your work I poorly read,
Scripted in a foreign tongue I do not fully understand,
But I glance at the typeset of your text,
Rising ghostly from the melancholy depths of the dusty oeuvre,
And am touched with pride and sadness.
They are words from another age,
Another era,
Steeped in blood and tragedy,
But they still speak to those who wish to hear.

Although you took that one last journey,
The road to Auschwitz,
You were not transient,
Died not your spirit,
For through your hard-wrought rhyme,
You reach us through the mists of atrocity,
A voice of majesty and power,
Articulating the common, working man with dignity,
Neither neglected nor forgotten.

I weep for you Adolf.
You are with sweetness within my consciousness preserved,
Though you died 'ere I lived.
My tears are for your inexpressible end
That was the cessation of our people,
The Hebrew,
Godly, ancient, cursed and blessed.

I gaze intensely at your likeness,
Aesthetic, spare,
Eyes of intellect, as they look through the years,
And I mourn.
I am uplifted yet humbled,
That courses through my veins,
As did yours,
The selfsame lifeblood of our fathers,
And that of our father's fathers,
Patriarchs all,
Our lineage uniting us in iron familial bond through time.
So long as I arise to walk another day,
And reach anew the setting of the sun,
In my bones, live you on.

02/09/2003

Written in memory of my cousin, Adolf Unger, Poet, 1904-1942,
who perished in Auschwitz on 13th September 1942.

THAT WE ENCOUNTERED ANGELS

Although remembrance is ephemeral,
Until I cease to be,
I recollect the thought of you
With tenderness.
As existence runs its course,
I gather sadness and euphoria in equal measure,
Encounter angels,
But just for now,
I stay my grieving,
Although one forfeits everything with time,
For nothing is forever.

We have each our temporal span,
As the scriptures say,
To sow and reap.
We touch unsurpassing love,
And are by sorrow decimated
As they take their leave of you,
One by one,
Their last farewells echoing in the mind,
As they infinite ascend,
Step high upon the sacred arc of Heaven.

They are my future and my past,
The quintessential flame,
Hot white,
And pure and crystal,
A star to blaze the way
As I thread through darkness.
At night's conclusion,
I raise my eyes to greet the sun,
Blinding in its glory,
Breathe in the oxygen of hope,
Gaze rapt upon the wonder of creation,
Its colour, form,
Its blessedness.

But one could never have it all,
Be cursed with every meretricious trifle one desires.
Just treasure minor blessings,
Be of gratitude for cherished souls
Enshrined in memory,
Both lost and gained,
Accept with grace and peaceful contemplation,
That the passing of the years
Denies us those for whom we mightiest care.

For the garlands and the grief of destiny,
Writ fire and gold in the Book of Life,
Are by a sager and a holier hand than I.
The loosening of the mortal coil
Is scripted in the skies with diamonds,
And however deep we mourn the loss
Of those who go before,
And weep,
They leave behind for us the greatest gift of all,
Divine remembrance,
That we encountered angels.

08/07/2004

TURN MY FACE TO THE WALL

I wait in humid silence for your call.
Should I metaphorically stretch out my hand
And have you touch it across the wire,
Or will you mentally retreat,
A fastidious man,
Distancing yourself in distaste at what I have become?

You are colder,
Indistinct,
In the midst of hiatus,
Almost unreachable at times,
Your noiseless, virtual footsteps echoing,
Then gradually ceasing inside my head,
Fading into eternity.

I thought it for life our mutual caring,
Reciprocal alliance.
Together, we would advance into the future unafraid,
For after all, we had the other.
Buoyed by the security of our bond,
Ectoplasmically linked,
We felt assured that if we stumbled,
There would be a shoulder to cushion our fall.

Perhaps no longer,
For I weaken,
Lose pride and dignity as l falter,
Become querulous, demanding,
Although it pains me to be so.
The imperfections of my psyche
Now overshadow our nexus,
As I crumble within, and peel without.
I drain your life-blood with my dark and leeching need,
So, choking on shame,
I turn my face to the wall.

03/09/2005

SIBLINGS

We never got along,
She and I,
Superficially chalk and cheese,
Although we were in truth
Both sides of the very same coin.

She was consumed by anger,
Bitterness
About her lot in life,
Believed she did not matter,
Was heartily disliked by many.
Perhaps a veracity of sorts,
But she was such a lost,
Pitiful little being,
Never able to emerge
From beneath my shadow,
I the star,
And she the duffer
She once heatedly declared.

I abandoned my sister,
Could do no other than escape,
Although I had little inkling
That she was in so desperate a place,
Facing mortality,

I kept my distance,
Fearful of her rages
And her paranoia.
We all did that in the end,
The family,
Walked away.

But now,
Although I have little detail
Of her sickness,
Her final days,
With profound sorrow I mourn,
Blood of my blood,
For I was not there
To offer comfort in her need,
So she passed away
With estrangement still between us.
I pray awaited her
Peace in another universe.

Such grief I hold,
For perhaps
I was all there once was
That belonged close to her heart
In testament,
Her indissoluble sibling.

22/09/2014

QUINTESSENCE

We come together,
Kin and friends,
To celebrate an auspicious day
Of unequivocal pleasure,
Birthday of
A quintessential being
Of rare spirit
And essence.

I could never attest
To be family,
Yet you gathered me in
As one of your own.
I shall always be other,
But you set for me
A place at your table,
Sanctuary.

Over these many years,
I have grown perhaps
To merit your kindness,
The compassion afforded
A once needy soul,
One aspiring still
To reciprocate,
With gratitude measureless,
Quiet affection

12/07/2016

This poem was written for Wendy Rosen, in celebration of her 70th birthday on 26 July 2016

GATEAUX

Patisserie,
Both an art
And a science of the soul,
A hallowed skill,
Holistic alchemy in the kitchen,
A mystical transmutation
From ragged, raw ingredient
To luscious gateaux.

I have honed to utter perfection
My plethora of recipes,
Mouthwatering concoctions,
Each to be devoured
In the sheer blink of an eye.

I prepare the cake with exhaustive effort.
It materialises
Ostensibly like magic,
Metamorphosis,
Then, whisked out of the oven,
And I gaze upon my ephemeral, blessed confection
As it cools,
With rapture.

I present my creation to an expectant clientele
Aglow with accomplishment, anticipation,
And silently enthuse
Those eagerly awaiting
My scrumptious masterpiece
To enjoy,
And I rejoice as they tuck in
With gratifying relish,
Savour each mouthful,
Indulge in one holy slice after another
Until all is gone, demolished,
Every crumb.

And I am on each occasion,
Suffused with pleasure
By my culinary triumph,
On rendering the consumers
Of my irresistible pièce de résistance,
Mightily replete,
With blissful content.

31/01/2013

VERTIGO

My heart constricted
As I watched them
Clamber out of the narrow window
Onto the forty foot drop,
For the neglected roof
Repointing required,
Expeditious repair.

It was imperative it be done
Ere winter set in,
And frosty weather,
Before the light faded,
The heavens darkened early into night.
It took fortitude, courage,
To tackle so vertiginous a task,
Way up high atop
The Georgian edifice.

Although they too,
Were apprehensive,
They set aside their concerns,
Addressed themselves to restoring
The sturdy, if elderly pile.
Not listed,
Nor even considered aesthetically pleasing,

But with an invincible soul,
Symbol of an era that erected
Such modest,
Yet innately elegant structures.

The undertaking, they pursued,
Over chilly autumn days,
With resolution,
Applying themselves
To the work in hand,
As engaged to do,
And to simply earn a crust.

I was apprised,
Intriguingly,
That the building possessed a chimney,
Had known that never before,
A romantic relic of the past,
I reflected,
Out of sight, redundant,
Yet still needful of attention
After all its venerable years.

So I fretted,
In a frenzy of trepidation
until they were through,
by anxiety eviscerated
as they tended to my domicile.

I thanked the roofers,
Almost welling up
With respect profound,
For their professional,
Honest,
Sheer old-fashioned expertise.
And valour.

07/11/2016

APOCALYPSE

The pain is disassociated,
In the head,
Not the heart,
For I have been here often,
Have become accustomed to the hollow ache,
The grievous longing and sense of loss in his absence.
It is futile to wish for better things,
Or listen vainly for the tintinnabulation
Of the telephone's skirl.

I offered all,
Corpus and spirit,
To have them on occasion incinerated by anguish,
The dread that some awesome apocalypse
Had befallen him again,
And indeed it was so.
I felt no singular premonition of disaster,
Could envisage only,
In the jagged silence,
in the void he left behind,
A destiny uncharted.

Where is he now
I ask the Heavens?
Far away,
In the midst of mortal conflict,
Hazard unforeseen?
Deep within the outer reaches of a twilit world
Where lesser beings seldom venture?
I take no comfort.

I wait still,
Without motion,
Draw barely a breath,
Contain a visceral sigh,
And pray wordless, in the hope it might be,
Not this time,
Not this time,
The knell tolls for thee.

07/08/2004

THE LILT OF THE ROSE

As the rose uncurled silken petal,
It rippled and shimmered.
The sweet-scented bloom
Hanging luscious and heavy,
Uplifted its crown and drank deep of the sun.

Blessed so it was by the beauty and wonder
Of the Earth and its greenery,
Its verdant lushness.
And as the flower listened to the wind,
And danced to its song,
To the Creator it bowed,
By whose hand the iridescent splendour before it
had been constructed.

As is the blossom perhaps blessed am I.
I was cursed I believed,
Imprisoned, forgotten, forsaken,
And was overcome by sorrow,
But damned was I never so,
For though,
As a corm 'neath the sod,
I grew without air,
My heart did not perish.
For despite the verity that love couples pain,
And one's benefactions are tempered by loss,
One must treasure always the holy gift of life.

And even though for me
The wait was so anguished,
So unendurably long,
More than half the span of my years,
As the rose in the wind,
I turned to the light.

So now and then,
Though but as a bud on the briar,
So quiet,
In my deep-buried self,
My soul gently spins
To the heartbeat of life.
And who knows,
Some day soon,
If, with uncertain ear,
I too shall listen to the wind,
And dance to its song.

13/02/2000

ARMAGEDDON

They observe the news,
Reports of warfare.
Oppressed become oppressor they assert,
Although Israel,
Gaza,
Each accelerate attrition.

Israel is compelled to struggle for survival,
A tiny, fragile scrap of land
In an ocean of aggressors.
It is all we have,
Sanctuary from the darkness of the Shoah.
Never again we pray,
But they do not heed.

Still no sanction
As the world implacably
Sets its face against the Hebrew,
The hate filled
And the conscience stricken
Equally free to vent their anger,
Covert anti-Semitism often
In the guise of righteousness.

And citing Hitler
As a man of rectitude,
Grieved he did not accomplish
The absolute decimation
Of my race.

Historical, irreconcilable loathing of the Jew
Still rampant.
It was ever thus,
And will endure
For death hath no dominion.

25/08/2014

SONNET

I penned the composition
With tender melancholy,
With such affection
It was almost without fault,
The most flawless
I shall ever set to paper,
And the kindest.

I read it to her,
Although I'd telephoned
To talk of other sad concerns,
Pedestrian woes,
But somehow,
The conversation veered
Toward my writing,
And that perfect rhyme.

She almost wept,
For it moved her deeply,
Its honesty and shining words
Recalled for her a friend
Who'd passed away.
It offered comfort,
And being powerful,
And a true verse,
It connected to her viscerally
In her grief,
Touched the recess of her heart.

So remember me,
The anonymous caller
At the end of the line
In the depths of the night,
Familiar,
Yet a stranger,
And do not forget my poem,
For perhaps I shall live on
If for no other reason,
Than a sonnet of love and loss.

01/01/2013

MATRIARCH

I think of her often,
With anguished deliberation.
It is many months since last we met,
And still I try to recall her
As once she was,
Vibrant,
Compassionate,
Supremely wise,
With diamond-sharp intellect.

I plan to see her soon
In the very last of her many homes,
A residence of note.
Not comfortless,
For she is impeccably cared for,
And it is quietly necessary
In the winter of her life,
That she be cosseted within
Such an orderly, practised, sheltering edifice.

I anticipate my visit
Will be one without solace,
For she is now profoundly consumed
By dementia.
When last I saw her,
She had retained a sliver of cognition,
Knew who I was,
But what now can I offer?
Grievously,
Her confusion has been swift and absolute
In its savage decimation.

Her luminosity dimmed,
The decline of the remarkable being
I so treasured,
To whom I owe my very survival,
Stains my heart
With indelible sadness.
The fading image
Of a once wondrous, all-encompassing Matriarch,
Unique,
Irreplaceable,
Is now but impetus for primal grief.

24/10/2011

BETWEEN BLOOD AND BONE

I look on,
A spectre at the feast.
I do not participate,
Merely observe as you effortlessly orchestrate your lives,
Navigate with ontological assurance.

I progress little,
Am evolved yet inchoate,
An autistic, inwardly focussed child,
Wordlessly constrained,
Communication a searing effort.
I shatter with ease,
Friable as sugar-spun crystal,
Eviscerated by minor exertion.

I cling to hope with a listless determination,
Gather up the shards of my fragile persona,
And inhale with care.
Each intake of breath is difficult, laboured,
Potentially bronchospasmic.
My odyssey is uncharted
As I vacuously follow the steps of Sysyphus,
Rolling the marbled onus ceaselessly over the horizon.

My optimism is a guttering flame,
Waxing and waning,
For blossom does not thrive in a dysfunctional garden.
With end-game desperation, I withdraw,
Seek refuge within that inner orifice next the heart,
Recede tightly dormant between blood and bone.

03/02/2006

OMI

I visualise her,
A Viennese Grande Dame,
Patrician,
With ringing, cut-glass timbre,
Steely, if fragile,
Remarkably lucid.

Immensely old
When she passed away,
A refugee from the Holocaust,
A memorable figure
From a bygone age.
I understand she did not suffer
When came the time,
On an afternoon, sitting sedately,
The following moment no longer sentient,
A gentle death.

Still of formidable intellect,
Memory selectively intact, if forgetful,
Questing,
Articulate, gregarious,
Empathetic,
A bestower of affection.

Despite only residual sight and hearing,
Even at so great an age
Discerning in her pursuits,
Attending lectures on art,
Finding solace in music.
She relished fine cuisine,
Although throughout her long existence,
Would roundly declare
She had yet to cook a morsel.

A striking presence,
Spare as a thoroughbred,
Which indeed she was,
Ramrod straight,
Hair neatly coiffed,
Arrayed in elderly but valeted attire,
Clutched to her side a Gucci bag,
Well worn, but of comfort.

So now,
Greta has left,
Marking the end of an era
For us all.
She had endured enough
Of life on Earth,
And who knows,
Perhaps aloft,
Still she is arranging matters
To her satisfaction,
In her very particular way.

07/12/2012

Written in memory of Greta Thaler-Kaye, who had a wonderful
life, and passed away very peacefully on 10/11/12, aged 98.

SERENDIPITY

A Utopian jewel,
Set neatly in a suburb to the east,
A modest Gothic pile.
Pacific, tranquil,
Fringed by luscious oasis,
Leafy, verdant, a riot of bloom.
It was a joyous, life-enhancing place to be,
With a gently, permeating ethos of humanity
That profoundly touched us all.
A matchless seat of healing
Of remarkable cohesion,
It functioned without effort,
A seamless, polished, smoothly-oiled machine.

We composed a disparate, melting pot of nations,
A diaspora of races,
An unaccustomed workforce for such xenophobic years,
Yet collectively we strove,
With pride and tempered harmony,
Coalescing into clan,
Indulgent, caring, tolerant of the others' foibles,
Imperfections,
A Gestalt,
A structure infinitely greater
Than its multitude of parts.

Around us,
As the monolithic, creaking giant,
The mighty NHS,
Was sinking slowly to its knees,
Splitting, crumbling, rent asunder
As politicians played,
We within the bubble of our magic, cosy serendipity
Worked on with vigour,
Blithe, regardless,
Sheltered,
Sublimely inattentive to the squall of breaking storms.

On reflection,
It seemed a Halcyon age,
Carefree,
Divinely blessed decades that quite transmogrified our lives.
As we decline and grey,
These long years since,
In a quiet corner of our consciousness
Still softly draws a cord of tensile strength,
Bonding us together in corporate entity.

Empathetic still,
And protective of our treasured gift,
The silken Gordian knot,
The unique and timeless sinew of fraternity that binds us
all,
Perennially,
We reunite in meetings almost holy in their warmth and
pleasure,
In celebration,
Appreciation undiminished,
Of our rare, enduring, peerless grail,
The grace upon each one of us bestowed,
The corona of our unity.

Dedicated with affection to all my ex-colleagues from the
London Chest Hospital 1973-1994.

23/10/2003

LUNATIC ASYLUM

In the kingdom of the riven mind,
Struck not the hour,
Time had ceased for those within.
Fogged existence,
Diurnal, soulless,
Void of meaning, love or joy.

Edifice of gothic graveyard stone,
Echoed to the tread of shuffling feet,
Our keepers malign, perverse,
Gauleiters, crude and cruel in their brutishness,
Keys at their side.
No need to wield the whip nor chain,
The pill, electrode, needle well sufficed.

A world lit dim.
Light filtered grey through motes of smoke,
A troubled place of murk and pain,
A fortress prison,
The inmates unholy and damned,
Forgotten, swallowed up in our abyss of despair.

Stood not one fierce, proud nor tall,
Nor straight of back,
But eyes cast low in our degradation,
Our souls shrivelled, shrunken,
Spiritless in the rusted cage inside and out,
On which smiled ne'er the star of hope.
Outcasts, pariahs,
Living out our sentences in penitence for the crime of
suffering,
Though not our suffering the crime.

08/03/1998

BUT WE SHALL NEVER FORGET HIM

Tiny, fragile,
Beset by pain,
Yet invincible in spirit.
With determined resolution
She contains her grief.
His departure beyond bearing,
She articulates her sorrow at his passing
With quiet dignity.

She reminisces wistfully,
But with humour,
With vivid recollection of their years together,
Has profound a need to talk of him
To assuage her sadness,
Lend her comfort,
Keep his memory alive.
But we shall never forget him.

Now comes the time for me
To give a little in return,
But it could never be enough,
For everything she offers
Is with such munificence,
So glad a heart.

25/07/2009

CIRCLE OF BRILLIANCE

I sit quietly,
Inarticulate, fragile, withdrawn,
Perched timidly on the periphery of your life.
An ill fit,
A mere spectator,
I am of minor consequence,
Intellectually lightweight.

I am never resentful,
Just a little forlorn
That I fall so far outside
Your magic, blessed circle of brilliance and privilege,
Yet am heartened
That still you extend me a welcome,
Judge me to be not entirely bereft of worth.

The absolute ease with which you dwell
Within your castle of perfection,
Furnished with such exquisite taste,
Fit so comfortably in your skin,
Inhabit your genius so unselfconsciously,
Mystifies me.

Born to inherit the universe,
Secure all prizes without effort,
Mirrored by your equally flawless offspring,
I marvel at your matchlessness.
How is it done,
To weave such a spell,
Glitter on?

25/09/2010

ENIGMA

I offer no answer,
If you lack understanding,
I cannot explain,
In the face of your anger,
Fares it better I turn
And hold silent my tongue,
For you question me harshly,
Perceive me unworthy,
But is the way of the world
And with time eases pain.

If you listen,
But hear not,
I shall not reprove.
I cannot condemn,
For it perhaps lies beyond
Mere perception of man.

Endless times have I passed
Through the eye of the storm,
Many more without doubt
Ere I journey at last
To the source for the cipher,
That enigmatic conclusion,
Beyond life
And hard reason.

03/02/2003

DECELERATION

As decline encroaches,
I no longer function
Tolerably well,
A perfunctory, second rate mind now,
Thought encumbered
By the passing of the years,
Falling silent in discourse
To disguise a fraying intellect.

A loosening grip on orderly life,
Ever the invalid
Whilst others thrive,
Exude optimal wellbeing,
In their prime still
As I,
If not quite retrogressing,
Decelerate.

Battling decay
As faculties fracture,
Groping for elusive, drifting words
To set down a rhyme,
Recall the past only through muddied shadow,
Attempt with futility
To conceal creeping deterioration,
Infirmity in all its pitilessness.

Hibernate to deflect
Derogatory opinion,
Disheartened as I observe my peers,
Their Utopian existence,
Seeming agelessness,
Perpetual vigour,
Yet asking of me,
Stoic quiescence.

07/09/2016

JACK AND THE CAULIFLOWER

It was to Forest Mere Health Farm that Esther was bound.
Before her departure,
For her Jack,
Her spouse of sixty-two years,
She conducted a tour of their well-stocked freezer.
Precise instructions were given,
Menus had been carefully prepared for dear Jack in her
absence.
He would not starve she was determined.
Elaborate dishes cooked and frozen,
Soups tasty and nourishing,
Meals for each day for his delectation and delight.

So Esther departed,
Confident that her Jack,
Her swan mate would not go hungry,
'Though she knew he would miss her greatly,
And pine for her return.

The week went by,
And Esther came home refreshed and revitalised.
What to find?
Her well-stocked freezer still well-stocked.
In fact, as packed with frozen dishes
As when she had made her exit to Forest Mere the week
before.
All the soups, tasty and delicious,
Still sitting there.
And each hearty gourmet spread, untouched and pristine.

With consternation and puzzlement, to Jack,
Esther turned.
Not a morsel had been eaten.
But why?
What on earth had Jack consumed in her absence,
If not the contents of their frozen larder, so lovingly filled?

Bemused, Esther asked,
'So what did you eat whilst I was gone Jack?'
Jack looked down at his feet.
'Toast'
'Toast!'
'Yes. toast,
Lots of toast,
You know l love toast.'
Esther stared at Jack, her heart sinking.
In a quavering voice, full of concern,
She said,
'And what else? What did you have for lunch?'

Jack looked sideways at Esther,
And with trepidation replied ,
'Cauliflower.'
'Cauliflower?' Esther squeaked.
'Yes', said Jack,
'Boiled cauliflower'.
'Boiled cauliflower Jack? Every day.
Boiled cauliflower?!'
'Yes, boiled cauliflower every day.
It was a very big cauliflower,
It lasted all week.'

Esther sat down heavily, and looked up at Jack.
'So what did you have, if anything,
To accompany your cauliflower?'
Jack, with hesitation, answered,
'Marks & Spencer's cauliflower cheese.
Very tasty, I enjoyed it very much.
It went quite well with the cauliflower,
'Though it didn't taste as good
As your lovely home cooking of course.'

Esther by now, felt quite faint.
Even the soups, hearty and nourishing,
Prepared with such loving care,
All still sitting neatly in a row in their capacious freezer,
Unconsumed.
'You didn't even touch the soups!' Esther reproached.
'No' said Jack in a strangled voice.
'Why not?' pleaded Esther.
'Well, you see' Jack muttered,
Hanging his head in shame.
'I kept forgetting to defrost them in good enough time
To empty into the saucepan.
It was so difficult trying to remember to do it.'

Esther gazed at Jack with pain in her eyes,
And said mournfully,
'So you didn't even have soup.'
Jack paused and then replied.
'Oh yes, I did have some soup.'
It was a knife in the heart,
And Esther, hurt beyond measure, sobbed.
'Soup, so you did have soup!
What soup, if not my lovely soup?'
Jack gulped and whispered,
'Heinz cream of mushroom soup.'

Esther shrieked as if the Heavens were about to fall in,
'Tinned soup! Soup from a can!'
Jack took a step backwards in alarm, and said fearfully,
'Yes, from a can. With toast.
It was really quite nice.
And it was so easy to open a tin.
No trouble at all.
I didn't even have to remember to defrost it first.'
And then added Jack in a deathly voice,
'And it did make a nice change from cauliflower
With Marks & Spencer's cauliflower cheese.'

08/03/1999

DACHAU

Only rarely have I reflected with intent
Upon the Holocaust,
Nor dared step on its soil
Even in nightmares,
Although I am an embodiment
Of the Jew
And child of a survivor,
Blood of blood,
Terrestrial DNA.

My father emerged from the abyss,
Enchained by its legacy,
Ever after only half alive,
Haunted as he lived on
With the horror,
Dark shadows of the savagery he witnessed,
Of the bloodshed visited
Upon his kindred,
Evil he took with him to the grave
In sequestered silence.

Psychotic,
Violent,
Obscene,
He could help none of it,
A tortured, innocent man,
Violated by the excoriating experiences
He sustained,
Memories of which to me
He never spoke,
Nor alluded.

Now I too as consequence,
Am burdened by the recall
Of his voiceless remembrance,
And his pain,
The scar incised upon his soul,
His riven mind,
And shall carry with me in turn
To the grave
His unexpressed terror,
Into life beyond death,
When approaches the time.

30/01/2014

NIRVANA

I watch it gentrify,
Observe its tentative metamorphosis
After a lifetime's residence
Of unremarkable domicile,
Witness the accelerating rise and rise
Of an ancient
If inconsequential
Quarter of the City.

I appreciate it,
Shabby yet historic,
Finds its essence and pedigree
Of endless fascination.
Once almost exclusively the domain of the poor,
Now stratified increasingly
By class and wealth,
If still fizzing with humanity.

Multicultural,
Transversed by artisans,
Diverse eateries,
Ubiquitous retail outlets
And independant businesses,
Jumbled markets,
Decaying council estates strafed by sporadic violence,
Yet graced here and there

By the beauty of a gothic edifice,
Arrondissements of affluence
Sequestered away down covert turnings.

Through a high casement,
I turn my gaze
To the conservation area arrayed below,
Interspersed by straits of trees,
At this optimal springtime semester
Burgeoning into leaf.

The transmutation of Walworth
Will come at cost for some,
And as the indigenous population is displaced,
The speculators snap up rapaciously
The neglected shops,
Period properties,
Sprouting new builds,
Enticed by the coy villaging,
Nascent gentrification,
The promise of this hitherto
Immutable bastion of the working class.

So it modulates,
An element within me
Gratified by the interest invested
In my quirky, undisciplined plot of the Metropolis,
At ease within my habitat,
Patch of the world,

Delighted by its modest blossoming,
But anxious that I too
Might no longer have the means
To reside upon the soil of this prospective Nirvana,
My comfortable life here
Dissipate like fairy dust
Into the ether,
Evanesce.

23/04/2014

REPENTANCE

Perhaps is the occasion
To reflect on my beliefs,
The role of my faith within the world,
Its tenets fundamental,
Endangerment reactivated.

Observing Yom Kippur
At the hallowed time,
Acknowledging again as I worship,
Atone for transgression,
That I be pure blood
Of the Hebrew,
To the Almighty shall ascend
When all is done.

Kinship as I sit
With fellow congregants,
Offering obeisance,
Although within the citadel of prayer
With few souls acquainted,
But still infused with emotion
As we stand in solidarity
On the most sacred,
Solemn of days.

Give thought as is custom
To forebears laid to rest,
Some,
Victims of barbarity,
In perpetuity mourned,
Their ultimate struggle for survival,
Beyond pity,
Yet I for now
Granted the freedom
To be who I am,
The Jew,
Unique, chosen, anointed.

Exult in the birthright
Elected upon me,
As scion
Of such ancient, proud,
Exalted bloodline.

22/10/2015

IN ABSENTIA

With gravity,
I reflected on her loss
In time of celebration,
Although the Chanukah soiree
Fell late this year.
In absentia now,
The cherished fellow diner,
An empty chair.

Bedecking the presents
With customary composure,
Purchased with affection
For my quasi, distant kin,
I considered,
There should be five,
Not four neat parcels,
And burgeoned again the melancholy
That she was gone,
Eternally,
The recipient for whom would be
The sumptuous gift.

As I wrapped,
I visualised the vacuum
Occasioned on her passing,
With lingering, potent sadness,
The light extinguished
By the exit
Of her maverick, feisty spirit,
Recalled the privilege,
And the pleasure
Of so inimitable an acquaintance.

Each Chanukah was the ritual
Of an annual presentation
Of my elegantly chosen gift.
She would welcome it
With delicate reservation,
Then effusively declare
It with a flourish,
In the very best of taste.

The effervescent social gatherings,
With Greta
At their heart,
Articulating wittily to empathetic guests,
And still in recollection,
I am touched,
Immensely gratified
To have delighted on occasion
So charismatic,
Resolute,
Loved a soul.

18/01/2014

A NIGHT AT THE OPERA

A stunning production
Of Lucia di Lammermoor,
On a chilly spring evening.
Of opera
An apotheosis,
Superlative,
Thrilling, unmatched,
The cast emoting as angels.

A dramatisation of controversy.
On the opening night,
An onslaught of boos and catcalls
For purported graphic content,
As reported in the Evening Standard.
What were we to witness,
We speculated,
Giggling,
How shocking could it be?

Before the performance,
We dined.
I had assiduously prepared
For my dearest of buddies,
A spectacular lunch,
Vichysoisse,
Coq au vin,

A delectable apple compote
With extra thick cream.
She enjoyed it immensely,
Enthusing,
Consumed it with relish.

We talked at length,
Gossiped, laughed,
Reminisced,
Spoke lovingly of absent old friends,
And then it was time
To set out
For our night at the opera.

As always,
The Opera House was a celebration
Of glittering, golden opulence,
The select audience
An elevated class,
Those enthroned in the costliest seats
A rarified breed,
Self-assured,
Expensively groomed,
In their natural habitat,
But for us a rare privilege.

The opera commenced
Amid much expectation.
The orchestra deeply bowed,
Clapped by us resoundingly.
It was peerless from beginning to end,
The soprano's soaring voice
Pure crystal,
Sweet as a nightingale,
The tenor's resonant, true,
All of it apiece,
The music an invention without equal
In the annals of opera canon,
Unbearably exquisite,
Sad beyond belief.

It was not distasteful
Of course,
The explicit parts as nothing,
Just genteel effort to update the production
A tad,
By which we were quietly amused,
Sat enthralled throughout
By the perfection of rendition
And music,
Speechless, transported.

It came to an end
After three exhausting hours.
From the audience,
An ovation of fifteen minutes
As they stamped their feet
And whistled,
Applauded thunderously.

We participated,
Equally carried away
On an occasion of magic, bejewelled melody,
Sublimely powerful,
Enchanting.

27/04/2016

ADIEU

She awaited their return,
To tender an unspoken farewell
Before she left,
An adieu to her kin,
Travelling far to her side
With imperative haste,
As she drew her last breath.
Shuttered down into absence now,
But tranquil,
For she had uttered,
If mutely,
The final parting.

I was with her
Ten days ere
That ultimate journey,
Diminished, gaunt,
Her power, charisma
And presence
No longer apparent,
Held tentatively her fractured hand,
Watched as shifted her eyes
Beneath lowered lids,
Responding perhaps infinitesimally,
Otherwise utterly still,
Quiescently composed.

With determination,
Perhaps she had selected
The time of departure,
Her soul hovering still,
Until the mysterious vacating of life
At the chosen hour.
With a quiet dignity of choice,
Had she made the binding decision
Of a gentle, resolute easing away
From the mortal world,
Only when all was done?

Written in memory of Esther Rosen MBE, an indomitable being, who passed away a few days before her 98th birthday.

28/01/2014

TOTEM

A latent member,
I observe the incineration
Of the movement,
Totem of democracy
Once voice of liberal debate,
Progressively silenced.

They do what they do
Without conscience,
The zealots,
Care little in their idol worship
Of the leader,
The golden calf,
The enabler
Of their totalitarian stranglehold
Upon the institution,
As moderate affiliates still dutifully
Pay their dues
Alongside the other bloating the membership,
Bent on furthering
The extreme hard left,
Its malevolent ideology.

They evince no lust for power
In the accepted sense,
Are a contradiction in terms,

For no one decent, rational could espouse their cause.
Only negatively they exist,
Obsess to liquidate,
Dismember, the Labour Party
Heart and soul,
Reconstruct it in their image
As the rump of the democratic faithful
Stand by,
Disempowered, sclerotic,
Unable to salvage it from immolation.

One hopes for resurrection
Sometime soon,
The day when circumstance
Defenestrates the brutish,
But little will is manifested currently
To stultify decay,
Preserve one's tempered optimism,
Idealistic expectation.

31/05/2016

IMAGES

They arrived by post,
Photographs of my antecedents
Collated by my sister.
Most butchered in the Holocaust,
Nameless,
Unreclaimed,
Close relatives,
Yet veiled in anonymity.

I struggle
To identify their faces,
Can merely place
My uncle,
And my father,
Young and lucid then,
Before incarceration
And subsequent psychosis,
Fresh faced,
Clear eyed,
Erect and solemn,
The cherished, youngest child.

I study them closely,
Portraits from another age,
Genteel,
Formal,
A time of false security.
The photographs emit an odour,
Faintly unpleasant,
Fruitily musty.
I touch them gingerly,
Speculate as to where
My sister might have stowed them,
To have them exsanguinate
Such redolence.

They speak without utterance,
Recount their fate in echoes,
Voiceless testament
Translocated in limbo,
Unquiet passing,
Suspended in eternity.

18/12/2015

TUTOR

Fragile, faltering,
Afflicted with a Dowager's Hump,
Yet fired with weary but buoyant determination,
Dancing intellect.
Quietly irrepressible,
With a coterie of friends
Attending folk festivals,
Folklore her especial passion,
Despite exhausting pain
And penury.

I could never be as she,
Half as doughty,
Such courage to carry on
Without capitulation,
Overcome almost insuperable disability.
She has even a little car,
Can perhaps,
Barely see over the dashboard,
Attests without it she would be grounded.

On occasion,
She waffles on a little,
But does not suffer from confusion,
Just finds everything
Requires such effort and stamina,
But is so disabled by her disorder,
Matters eviscerate and flummox her at times,
But one must be patient,
For if one listens hard,
Once she has settled,
She abounds with nuggets of cultural wisdom,
Ideas of an esoteric nature,
As she peers at us over her glasses
With wise, enquiring eyes.

In her halcyon days,
She was doubtless
A force to be reckoned with,
Someone quite special,
Perhaps even straight of back,
And still, if with difficulty,
Did what she did
With distinction, I believe.
Her poetry is far finer than mine,
Seemingly effortless and perfect,
A gifted soul,
A naturally fine mind,
If overburdened with age and ague.

As I get to know her
More intimately,
My respect and affection for her
Grow,
As do that of others.
Indeed,
She is overwhelmed by officialdom,
Subsumed by their empathy.

Her teaching is one of a kind,
Off the wall,
Motivating one toward
Another, uncharted dimension,
Encouraging one to strive to be
A more accomplished writer,
Attempting the arduous,
Produce work of quality more profound.

Lately,
I have begun to prepare my fabled cakes
For our creative writing class,
And they tuck in with gusto.
Her eyes light up discreetly
As she beholds my creation,
Anticipating taking home the remainder,
Would be crestfallen if denied,
Nibbles it zestfully
As she perches with discomfort
In her miniscule, disordered flat,

Without a bean to make it smarter,
But her pleasure in my baking
Delights me hugely.

I wish her so well,
Esteem her mightily
In her battles with the world,
Her feisty spirit,
And thank her without,
I hope,
Embarrassing articulation,
For enthusing one
With novel, literary invention.

10/11/2015

HOLY GRAIL

Lies it deep within,
Salvation,
The holy grail,
The sceptred gate to freedom?

From birth
I knelt in shadow,
For they stood far beyond reach,
And rocked not the infant,
Sustained not the child,
Nor comforted the woman.

Although I ache to don
The shimmering robe
Of the perfect,
Bonded soul,
With sinew strong,
And mind of crystal,
Must I accept with grace
The fate spelt out for me
In the nebulous,
Glancing stars.

06/11/2001

INIMITABLE WALWORTH SOCIETY

Despite the chill,
It was compelling
To follow the debate
Of the Walworth Society,
Two hours of issues
Relating to its existence,
Reason to be.

The meeting took place
As is customary,
In the exquisite St. Peter's Church,
In the depths of winter
On this occasion,
A monthly assembly I rarely attend,
Feel morally guilty
Not being present more often,
A gathering devoted
To matters Walworth.

The members are primarily
The Bourgeoisie,
With a minority
Of indigenous working-class residents,
But all equally passionate
In their attachment
To our cherished locale.

Our patch of London
Was once elegant,
Fashionable, in days gone by,
Is still historically significant.
Stalwarts of the Society
Volunteer their time
For exhaustive research,
Striving to preserve
And collate
Walworth's every notable aspect,
Edifice, byway,
Pub, artefact.

I too harbour for it
An affection,
For it is special,
Unique in character,
Bustling, thriving, despite hard times,
With a strong beating heart,
Gentrifying now
If still rough around the edges,
But of consequence.

So I listened intently,
Shivering in the cold,
Marvelling at their formidable efforts
On behalf of Walworth,
Indefatigably battling
To rescue the post office,
Town Hall,
Amid tackling other relevant concerns.

Manifesting the role they play
In the flourishing of the rich meld
Of artistry, culture and activity,
All alive and well within the nucleus
Of our robust, urban,
Singular milieu.

12/02/2017

SYNDROME

A freakish malaise,
This dark dream of body and mind.
Such razor sharpness of sense and feeling,
Every nerve, muscle, thought,
So finely,
So painfully attuned.
Bizarre,
Unique.

It settled hard on my shoulders so young,
The frightful onus I would ever carry.
It ate into my heart,
Engulfed,
Devoured my psyche,
Imprisoned my soul,
My spirit,
Drained my bodily strength.
Was I predestined to be born
So aching,
So poorly,
So burdened,
So overwhelmed by the misery,
The pain of it all.

Or did it grow by chance,
Unbidden,
Nestling like an incubus,
And then,
When the evil time was come,
Spring forth fully formed and diabolical?
So must I live with my demon,
Accommodate it and its deathly presence,
Exhausting and fearful.
A cannibal,
Tearing and feeding,
Sucking dry in its greed.

And yet,
Like a dark star,
A black diamond,
Am I entirely cursed?
Within the palsied shell,
Creative and dancing,
My mind,
Though frenetic and ill,
Still effulgent and sparkling.

Despite hurt and despair,
My spirit burns brighter and fiercer,
My love,
Though more anguished,
The greater.

05/10/1999